EDGE
BOOKS

The Unexplained
The Loch Ness Monster

by Terri Sievert

Consultant:
Dr. Robert Rines, President
Academy for Applied Science
Concord, New Hampshire

Capstone
press

Mankato, Minnesota

Edge Books are published by Capstone Press
151 Good Counsel Drive, P.O. Box 669, Mankato, Minnesota 56002
www.capstonepress.com

Library of Congress Cataloging-in-Publication Data
Sievert, Terri.
    The Loch Ness monster / by Terri Sievert.
        p. cm.—(Edge books. The unexplained)
    Includes bibliographical references and index.
    ISBN 0-7368-2716-1 (hardcover)
    1. Loch Ness monster—Juvenile literature. [1. Loch Ness monster. 2. Monsters.]
I. Title. II. Series.
QL89.2.L6S54 2005
001.944—dc22   2003026407

Summary: Describes the sightings of and the search for the Loch Ness monster.

Editorial Credits
Angela Kaelberer, editor; Juliette Peters, designer; Kelly Garvin, photo researcher;
    Eric Kudalis, product planning editor

Photo Credits
Cover photo: Fortean Picture Library/Anthony Shiels. This photo was taken from
Urquhart Castle on May 21, 1977. Its authenticity has not yet been proven.

Copyrights Josef Moravec, Prehistoric World Images, 18
Corbis/Bettmann, 9, 15; Ralph White, 7; Reuters NewMedia Inc., 23
Elijah Erkelino, 28, 29
Fortean Picture Library, 12; Austin Hepburn, 25; Hamish M. Brown, 13;
    Hugh Gray, 11; Nicholas Witchell, 19; Project Urquhart, 20; R. K. Wilson, 26
Getty Images Inc./Hulton Archive, 5, 16

1 2 3 4 5 6 09 08 07 06 05 04

Table of Contents

Chapter 1

Something in the Loch

In March 1933, Mr. and Mrs. John Mackay were driving on a road near a lake called Loch Ness in Scotland. They saw something big, black, and shiny moving in the lake.

Mr. Mackay parked the car. The couple watched a creature roll and plunge in the water. The Mackays said the creature made waves the size of those made by a large ship.

Learn about:
- A frightening sight
- The creature on land
- A deep, dark lake

In the early 1930s, a new road allowed people to drive around Loch Ness.

The Loch Ness Monster

In July 1933, Mr. and Mrs. George Spicer were driving along the southern bank of Loch Ness. They saw something that looked like a huge snail near the road. It had a long neck, a thick body, and four flippers.

The Spicers said the beast trudged out of the brush on the side of the road. It carried a small animal in its jaws. The creature crossed the road and went through the brush into the lake.

Loch Ness

Loch Ness is in the hills of northern Scotland. The Ness River and the town of Inverness are at the north end of the lake. Loch Ness also forms part of the Caledonian Canal. This waterway connects the Atlantic Ocean with the North Sea.

The lake is long, narrow, and deep. It is 23 miles (37 kilometers) long and 1 mile (1.6 kilometers) wide. The water is about 750 feet (229 meters) deep.

The lake's water is dark and cloudy. Rivers and streams carry pieces of decayed plant material called peat into the lake. People can only see about 6 feet (1.8 meters) below the water's surface.

Sightings of a strange animal in Loch Ness have been reported for at least 1,500 years. Some people believe the animal is real. Others say people mistake natural objects for an animal.

⬇ Loch Ness is one of four lakes that are connected by the Caledonian Canal.

Chapter 2

History and Legend

Few people outside the Loch Ness area knew about the mysterious sightings until the 1930s. In 1933, a new road was built on the north shore of Loch Ness. The road made it easier for people to drive around the lake. Rocks, trees, and barrels fell into the water as the road was being built. Some people say the noise made the monster come out of the lake.

Learn about:
- Early sightings
- Photo proof
- New interest

Rocks and other objects fell
into Loch Ness when the road
was built around the lake.

Gathering Interest

In 1933 and 1934, many people came to Loch Ness to look for the monster. In 1933, writer Rupert Gould talked to about 50 people who said they had seen the creature.

Gould learned that most of the sightings were on warm, calm days. Most people said they saw something that looked like an upturned boat. Others said the creature had a long neck and head.

Photo Evidence

People wanted more proof that the monster existed. Hugh Gray gave it to them in 1933. He took a picture of the beast.

Gray's unclear photo shows what looks like a snake moving in the water. Gray said the creature was 40 feet (12 meters) long with a thick tail and rounded back.

In 1934, Sir Edward Mountain brought 20 people to Loch Ness to look for the monster. The people watched the water 10 hours each day for five weeks. They reported 20 sightings of the monster and took five photos. These photos were printed in the *Illustrated London News.*

On April 1, 1934, Dr. R. K. Wilson took the most famous photo of the monster. The photo clearly shows a head and neck coming out of the lake. He said the creature's neck was 6 feet (1.8 meters) long. Wilson gave the photo to the *Daily Mail* newspaper in London. Many other newspapers later published the photo.

▲ In November 1933, Hugh Gray took the first photo of the Loch Ness monster.

After 1934, many people lost interest in the monster. Some people thought witnesses made up the sightings. People had other worries as well. Scotland and the rest of the United Kingdom soon entered World War II (1939–1945).

Rebirth of a Legend

In the 1950s, Constance Whyte brought back interest in the Loch Ness monster. Whyte talked to many people who said they had seen the monster. She wrote a book about the sightings.

After Whyte's book was published, searchers brought underwater cameras and sonar equipment to the lake. Sonar uses sound waves to detect objects. In 1957, sonar suggested that a large creature lived in the lake. But no physical proof was found.

MORE THAN A LEGEND
The Story of the Loch Ness Monster
by Constance Whyte

▲ Whyte's book brought new interest in the monster.

Loch Ness Legends

About 1,500 years ago, people called Picts lived in Scotland. They carved pictures of animals into the stones around Loch Ness. One of the beasts has a spout or flipper coming out of its head. Some people think this carving is an early picture of the Loch Ness monster.

Around the same time, people told stories about Saint Columba. Columba was a Christian missionary who stopped at Loch Ness. The story says Columba saw a beast that looked like a huge frog. The animal was about to swallow a man who was swimming in the lake.

The story then says that Saint Columba raised his hand. He ordered the beast to go away. The creature fled. The swimmer was saved.

Ancient Pict carvings were found near Loch Ness.

Chapter 3

Searching for a Monster

Engineer Tim Dinsdale began researching the monster sightings in 1959. In 1960, Dinsdale said he filmed the monster. His short movie shows two humps rising out of the water. The creature zigzags before going under the water. It then surfaces and makes large waves. Dinsdale said the animal moved at about 10 miles (16 kilometers) per hour.

Members of the United Kingdom's Royal Air Force studied Dinsdale's film. They said the movie probably showed a living creature.

Learn about:
- A monstrous film
- Sonar searches
- Flipper photo

40-50 FT.

...TER BASED ON ANALYTICAL STUDY OF THE EVIDENCE.

In 1960, Tim Dinsdale used his sighting of the monster to make a model of the creature.

▲ In 1969, scientists used a small submarine to
search for the Loch Ness monster.

Sonar and Submarines

The first large scientific studies of Loch Ness took place in 1960 and 1962. A group from Oxford and Cambridge universities in England used cameras and sonar to search the lake. Their sonar found a large, moving underwater object. No one knows for sure what it was.

In 1968, a team from Birmingham University in England set up a sonar system near the lake. The sonar tracked two objects that rose and dived quickly. Again, no one was certain what they were.

The next year, researchers searched the lake with a small submarine, divers, and sonar. They found no evidence of the monster.

Other Searches

In 1970, a team from the Academy of Applied Science in Concord, New Hampshire, came to Loch Ness. Robert Rines led the search.

The researchers set up an underwater camera in the lake. It took a picture every 45 seconds. On August 8, 1972, the camera took a photo of an object. Rines used a computer to make the photo clearer. It showed what looked like the tail and part of a flipper of a large animal. Rines thought the flipper was 6 to 8 feet (1.8 to 2.4 meters) long.

Animal expert Sir Peter Scott said the creature in the photo looked like a plesiosaur. This reptile lived between 200 million and 65 million years ago during the time of the dinosaurs.

▼ Some people believe the monster is a plesiosaur.

In October 1987, Operation Deep Scan used 19 boats equipped with sonar to study the lake. The sonar made three contacts with an object larger than a shark and smaller than a whale. The object was larger than any animal known to live in a lake.

▲ **The boats of Operation Deep Scan searched the deepest area of Loch Ness.**

Recent Findings

Project Urquhart began in 1992. Researchers studied the lake's shape. They also studied the plants and animals living in the lake. The researchers' sonar showed a large object.

▼ Project Urquhart researchers studied the plants and animals in Loch Ness.

It was larger than the fish known to live in the lake. The researchers also counted the fish living in the lake. They found that not enough fish live in the lake to feed a large animal.

In 2003, a team working with the British Broadcasting Corporation (BBC) searched the lake. The team used 600 sonar beams and satellites. The researchers found only a buoy trapped under the water.

The researchers said that people imagine the sightings. To test this idea, the researchers placed a fence post in the lake. A group of tourists were near the lake. The researchers raised the post out of the water. They asked the tourists to draw what they saw. Most of the tourists drew figures that looked like fence posts. Only a couple of people drew heads shaped like monsters.

Chapter 4

What Could It Be?

Some people believe that the Loch Ness monster is a plesiosaur that somehow survived whatever killed the dinosaurs. Plesiosaur fossils have been found in and near Loch Ness.

In July 2003, Gerald McSorley tripped over a fossil in the water near the lake's shore. The fossil was part of the backbone and spinal cord of a plesiosaur. The National Museum of Scotland said the fossil was about 150 million years old. It came from a creature that was 35 feet (11 meters) long.

Learn about:
• Plesiosaurs
• Hoaxes
• Recent sightings

In 2003, Gerald McSorley found part of a plesiosaur fossil near the shore of Loch Ness.

Natural Explanations

The mist that hangs over Loch Ness can make ordinary objects look odd. Alex Campbell thought he saw the monster in 1933. He later said that he may have seen birds in the mist.

Some people believe the monster is an ocean animal that entered the lake when the Ness River was high. They think the monster is a giant eel, a shark, or a whale. Others think people mistake otters or seals for the monster.

Objects in the lake could be mistaken for the monster. These objects include logs, plants, and clumps of peat. Waves can look like a monster's hump in the lake.

Fact or Hoax?

Some people say the Loch Ness monster is a hoax. They say people made up stories about the monster to attract tourists to the area.

A newspaper hired Marmaduke Wetherell to search for the animal in 1933. He said he found footprints made by a large animal. A few weeks later, experts from the British Museum said a stuffed foot from a hippopotamus made the footprints.

▲ Some people think this 1996 photo shows the monster's hump. Others think it shows only waves.

In 1994, researcher Alastair Boyd said he had proof that R. K. Wilson's famous photo was a fake. Boyd's story came from Christian Spurling, who was Marmaduke Wetherell's stepson. Spurling said he put a gray head and neck on a toy submarine. Wetherell and another man put the fake monster in the lake

▲ The most famous photo of the Loch Ness monster was taken in 1934.

and took a picture of it. Wetherell then gave the photo to Wilson.

Not everyone believes the photo is a fake. Some researchers say a toy submarine could not have supported the head and neck. A second photo was taken right after the first. This photo shows the monster in a different position than the first photo. These people believe the photos prove a monster once lived in Loch Ness.

More Sightings

People continue to report sightings of the monster. In May 2001, James Gray and Peter Levings were fishing on the lake. Gray saw something in the water and took a photo. The men said the creature raised itself slightly, arched forward, and went underwater. It had a long black neck.

In August 2002, Roy Johnston took several photos of a creature in the water. He said the creature was about 7 feet (2 meters) out of the water. It looked like a large snake.

A New Expedition

In August 2003, Robert Rines led another group of researchers to Loch Ness. This time, the researchers looked for bones or other remains of the monster.

The research crew used a Remotely Operated Vehicle (ROV) to search the lake.

▼ In August 2003, Robert Rines (left) and his crew searched for remains of the monster.

▲ Rines' 2003 expedition used a Remotely Operated Vehicle to search Loch Ness.

They lowered the ROV beneath the lake's surface. The ROV sent images from the lake and the lake's floor to the crew. The researchers found the remains of an ancient ocean bed under the lake. They didn't find any bones or other remains of the monster. Rines and his crew plan to keep searching until they solve the mystery of the deep, dark lake.

Glossary

flipper (FLIP-ur)—an armlike body part that an ocean or freshwater animal uses to swim

fossil (FOSS-uhl)—the remains or traces of something that once lived; bones and footprints can be fossils.

hoax (HOHKS)—a trick to make people believe something that is not true

loch (LAHK)—a lake in Scotland

peat (PEET)—partly decayed plant matter found in swamps

plesiosaur (PLEE-see-uh-sohr)—a large reptile that lived during the time of the dinosaurs

sonar (SOH-nar)—a device that uses sound waves to find underwater objects; sonar stands for sound navigation and ranging.

tourist (TOOR-ist)—a person who travels and visits places for fun or adventure

Read More

Delrio, Martin. *The Loch Ness Monster.* Unsolved Mysteries. New York: Rosen, 2002.

Gorman, Jacqueline Laks. *The Loch Ness Monster.* X Science. Milwaukee: Gareth Stevens, 2002.

Streissguth, Thomas. *The Loch Ness Monster.* Mystery Library. San Diego: Lucent, 2002.

Internet Sites

FactHound offers a safe, fun way to find Internet sites related to this book. All of the sites on FactHound have been researched by our staff.

Here's how:

1. Visit *www.facthound.com*
2. Type in this special code **0736827161** for age-appropriate sites. Or enter a search word related to this book for a more general search.
3. Click on the **Fetch It** button.

FactHound will fetch the best sites for you!

Index